we

Neli Nathan

BookLeaf Publishing

India | USA | UK

we © 2023 Neli Nathan

All rights reserved.

No part of this publication may be reproduced, stored in a retrieval system, or transmitted, in any form or by any means, electronic, mechanical, photocopying, recording or otherwise, without the prior written permission of the presenters.

Neli Nathan asserts the moral right to be identified as author of this work.

Presentation by *BookLeaf Publishing*

Web: www.bookleafpub.com

E-mail: info@bookleafpub.com

ISBN: 9789358316247

First edition 2023

DEDICATION

to us for getting this done <3

PREFACE

Doctor Who
Season 2
Episode 10
39:13

forbidden love

you cannot love her
for it is sin

but you have not seen the way
my name rolls off her tongue

you have not felt the way
her skin brushes mine

but if heaven lives within her
i'll take the chance of sin

too beautiful for earth

you and i both lost
more than i can ever gain again

now the only thing i can do
is prepare myself
for the day i get to hear you say my name

false truths

as a child
i was always told that when a boy is mean to you
he must like you

i guess that is why
when you so violently caressed my skin
i convinced myself to stay

ghosts

how am i supposed to move on
when i am haunted by all the things you are

you

5

there was no you to hold
there was no you to kiss
there was no you to caress
there was no you
so how is it possible i am grieving a you i will
never get to meet

intimacy

he touched me

without ever touching me

jealousy

i envy the rains
who still get to caress you

robbed innocence

my breasts have been drained of its sweetness

for melons of vinegar is all i have left

now

9

you are everywhere
except right here

te quiero

if i die before you
i'll come visit you through butterflies

and if i go first
i'll see you through all the stars
in the sky and all the love you feel

Gone

11

I never saw you become a man,
you never saw me become a good one.
You are long gone, but I'll work to be all that
you were

The March

The march, led by fools and thieves .
Into the black,
we know not another way.
The truth is shielded, we fear.
For when the world is black
Who can say they stand in the light?

Fight

Hearts and fists pounding,
sounds of cheers or fear.
Blood and sweat, and
the only place I feel at home

Nights

14

It was late nights and early mornings,
all gathered around a pipe.
Hours and days and weeks in a session.
Crowded rooms, and we were all alone

Can't

Here and there, I just can't do it.
Now and then, I don't want to.
Lost jobs and dreams and friends.
They all went with the wind, and,
sometimes, I want that too

Brothers

Band of Brothers,
but the band broke up

Eyes

17

I got your eyes, your patience, and your strength.
Maybe that's why I'm always trying to save

Weird

I was born weird,
which is a gift,
I see things you look past

Mom

I see the way you love my dad,
and I've seen his past.
I'm glad he found you, at last

Eyes

Her eyes are like the time I died, and her laugh
is like when I came back to life

She

21

She is everything love should be,
I just wish she could see

www.ingramcontent.com/pod-product-compliance
Lightning Source LLC
LaVergne TN
LVHW050304200726
843509LV00015B/3147